Who Best To Speak For Me, Than Me?
My Last Wishes Guide

Ms. Paulique M. D. Horton

Horton and Associates Financial Services

Table of Contents

Declaration Page

My Prayer is that this guide will help you through life's hardest times which is my death. Often it doesn't matter how much we try to prepare these are the most difficult moments to navigate through and this guide will help with some of that.

Try your best to carry out my final wishes.

Please know I love you dearly and I appreciate you with all my heart!

Signed:

_____

Personal Information

Full Name:

_____

Maiden Name:

_____

Address:

_____

_____

Previous Address (if new address less
than 5 years):

_____

_____

_____

Social Security Number:

Birthplace:

Birthdate:

Citizenship:

Resident Since:

Current Occupation:

Since:

Previous Occupation:

Employer:

Employer Telephone Number:

Date Employed:

Previous Employer (If less than 5 Years):

Highest Level of Education:

College (Explain Degree & Greek affiliation if applicable):

Marital Status:

Spouse:

Name of Father:

Father Place of Birth:

Name of Mother:

Mother Place of Birth:

Current Primary Physician:

Current Attorney (Name and Telephone Number):

Veteran's Record (If applicable):

Location of Important Documents

Keep **this book** separate from Important Documents, allow this guide to direct our loved ones and not burglaries to the location of the important documents

Birth Certificate:

_____

Children/Grandchildren Birth
Certificate (If Applicable):

_____

_____

_____

Marriage Certificate:

_____

Divorce Certificate (if Applicable):

_____

Will and Testament (Is it filed with your
local register of deeds office?):

_____

_____

Deeds:

....

Stocks and Bonds:

....

Military Records:

....

Automobile Title/Lien:

....

Retirement Plan:

....

Executive Order:

....

....

Address Book:

_____

_____

Life Insurance Policies:

_____

_____

Bank(s) Account(s)

_____

_____

Register/Accounts/Statements:

_____

_____

_____

_____

_____

_____

Companies to Notify

1. Life Insurance Company(ies)

Name:

_____

Policy Number:

_____

Telephone Number:

_____

Policy Number:

_____

Telephone Number:

_____

Beneficiary (Primary and Secondary):

Name:

_____

_____

_____

_____

_____

_____

_____

_____

_____

_____

_____

_____

_____

_____

_____

_____

2. Bank(s)

Name(s):

_____

_____

_____

Telephone Number:

_____

Account Number:

_____

_____

_____

_____

_____

_____

_____

Beneficiary (Please remember to list
Beneficiaries on all bank and investment
accounts):
Name(s):

_____

_____

_____

_____

Telephone Number:

_____

Account Number:

_____

_____

_____

_____

_____

_____

_____

_____

3. Retirement Plans (Accounts)

Name:

_____

_____

Telephone Number:

_____

Account Number:

_____

_____

Beneficiary:

_____

_____

Employer

_____

_____

_____

_____

Name:

Telephone:

Human Resource or Benefit
Telephone Number:

4. Investment Companies Name:

_____

_____

Telephone Number:

_____

_____

Account Number:

_____

_____

_____

_____

_____

_____

_____

_____

_____

Assets

Banks Accounts:

_____

_____

_____

Bank Name

_____

_____

_____

Type of Account

_____

_____

_____

Account

_____

_____

_____

Addresses of Property Owned:

_____

_____

_____

_____

_____

_____

_____

_____

_____

_____

Credit Cards:

Company Name

Type

Card Number

Safe Deposit Box:

_____

_____

Coin Collection:

_____

_____

Art:

_____

_____

Cryptocurrency:

_____

_____

_____

_____

_____

Life Insurance Policies where you are the policy owner of:

_____

_____

_____

Other:

_____

_____

_____

_____

_____

_____

_____

_____

_____

_____

Funeral/Memorial Service

Following are my wishes and desires for my Funeral/Memorial.

Funeral Director/Home of Choice:

_____

_____

_____

Location of Service:

_____

_____

_____

_____

_____

Location of Repass:

_____

_____

Church Membership/Affiliation:

_____

_____

_____

Casket or Cremation:

_____

Casket Clothing and Accessories:

_____

_____

_____

_____

_____

Special Musical Selections and/or
Soloists:

_____

_____

_____

_____

_____

_____

_____

_____

_____

_____

_____

_____

_____

Pictures (location/description) to use for
Announcement, Service, and Obituary:

_____

_____

_____

_____

_____

_____

_____

_____

_____

_____

_____

_____

_____

_____

_____

Cemetery

Preferred Interment:

○ Earth Burial

○ Mausoleum

○ Cremation

Name of Cemetery:

_____

_____

City & State:

_____

_____

_____

_____

Own Cemetery Property or Prepaid of Plot (Location):

_____

_____

_____

Permit Needed: ○ Yes ○ No
Type of Property:

_____

_____

_____

Arrangement Preferred (Specify family estate, two persons, or single):

_____

_____

_____

_____

_____

Headstone

....

....

....

Company:

....

....

....

Prepaid for Services: ○ Yes ○ No
Description of Headstone:

....

....

....

....

....

....

....

....

For cremation describe final wishes of remains:

_____

_____

_____

_____

_____

_____

_____

_____

_____

_____

_____

_____

_____

Other Requests:

_____

_____

_____

_____

_____

_____

_____

_____

_____

_____

_____

_____

_____

_____

_____

Obituary

Please write out obituary. Better to be prepared than not. Loved ones prefer this to be ready. But remember deceased relatives, all affiliations, and dates.

_____

_____

_____

_____

_____

_____

_____

_____

_____

Obituary Continued

Obituary Continued

Obituary Continued

Username & Password (Passcode) List

Passcode To Computer(s):

_____

_____

_____

Passcode To Cellphone and Tablets:

_____

_____

_____

_____

ATM or Bank Card Pin Code:

_____

_____

_____

Username and Passcode to Online

Banking:

_____

_____

_____

Username and Passcode to Credit Card

Websites:

_____

_____

_____

Username and Passcode to Employee

Company Log In:

Username and Passcode to Investment

Websites:

Username and Passcode to Social Media
Platforms (List All):

_____

_____

_____

_____

_____

_____

Username and Passcode to Virtual
Wallet and Cryptocurrencies:

_____

_____

_____

_____

_____

Username and Passcode to ALL eBill Pay
Companies (Example, cellular phone
company, electric company, any home
utilities you pay electronically.

Moments of Reflection

What has life meant to you?

_____

_____

_____

_____

_____

_____

_____

_____

_____

_____

Things you remember the most?

What are you most grateful for?

What are your biggest prayers?

What are the few things you want to be
remembered by?

Your favorite place to visit or travel?

What is (are) your favorite saying(s)?

A Special Note to
Family and Friends

Funeral, Memorial and Contact Checklist

☐ Call Relatives & Friends-Find Address Book

☐ Call Coroner or Doctor

☐ Call Funeral Director or Funeral Home

☐ Call Insurance Agent or Insurance Company

☐ Notify Church, Minister or Pastor

☐ Call Co-workers and social organizations

☐ Call Life Insurance Companies that "I" was the Policy Owner of

☐ Notify Banks, Investment Accounts, and Retirement Accounts

☐ Choose Funeral location and Cemetery location if applicable

☐ Choose Casket or Urn

☐ Choose Clothing and Accessories

☐ Choose Flowers and Flower Spread

☐ Choose Music, Soloists and Funeral Program Participants

☐ Choose Repass Location and Menu

☐ Choose Announcement Cards and Thank you Cards

☐ Choose Location for Family gatherings throughout the funeral and memorial process

☐ Order Death Certificates from Funeral Home or Director

Notes

Notes

Notes

Notes

Made in the USA
Monee, IL
07 November 2020

46853133R00035